STEAM PACKET IN *Camera*

Published by:

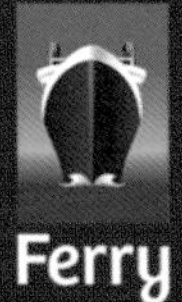

Ferry Publications, PO Box 33,
Ramsey, Isle of Man IM99 4LP

Tel: +44 (0) 1624 898446 Fax: +44 (0) 1624 898449

E-mail: ferrypubs@manx.net
Website: www.ferrypubs.co.uk

Stan Basnett

Foreword

The sea, together with the ships that sail upon it, has long been a fruitful source of inspiration to artists and in more recent times, photographers have found it a compelling subject to record.

It's not just the beauty and awesome majesty of the sea – whether calm or raging – but also the grace of the ships that ply on it, and the mystique of the men and women who entrust themselves to the wind and waves to ensure that their vessels reach a safe mooring at the end of the voyage.

Stan Basnett's latest volumes of photos of the life and times of the Steam Packet – mainly his photos, but also many taken by others – is not just his perspective on that source of inspiration, but also a fascinating record of the Company and its fortunes, as well as a social history of the community it has served so faithfully for over 180 years.

The period covered in *Steam Packet in Camera* – from 1930 to the present day – sees a transition from the extensive fleet of sleek, graceful steam turbine powered greyhounds of the middle years of the 20th century (the fast craft of their day) to the more utilitarian though still appealing multi-purpose ferries that cater for the needs of the modern consumer, and most recently to the Company's latest acquisition, *Manannan,* a vessel capable of 41 knots and a cruising time to Liverpool of 2½ hours. It also reflects changes in consumer expectation from slatted wooden seats on open decks, silver service dining rooms and ladies only lounges with a resident nurse – to air-conditioned luxury lounges with aircraft style seating and on-board entertainment. Through it all we glimpse not only the backdrop of the Isle of Man, itself a source of inspiration and an object of affection to so many, but also some more unfamiliar backdrops. In the background we see the officers and crews of the Steam Packet, whose devotion to duty and finely honed skills, combine to ensure that the ferry almost always gets through, even in the most hostile conditions.

The record charts turbulent times as well – from the disaster of Dunkirk, when three of the Company's vessels were lost together with irreplaceable crew members – through times of near suicidal competition which nearly brought the Company to its knees to the first decade of the 21st Century when a slimmed down, fit for purpose fleet designed to meet the Isle of Man's specific needs, shuttles across that narrow stretch of sea which defines our Island home.

Robert Quayle

The Steam Packet is indivisible from the community it serves – the Isle of Man. Exciting fierce pride at times and frustration at others – the Company is recognised as an institution which manages to meet the challenges it faces and maintain its services whatever obstacles it has to overcome.

Stan Basnett and fellow enthusiasts have provided us with evocative pictures of the ships which are the Island's lifeline. Those photos will remind us not only of times past – but also of the commitment and service that have contributed so much to the Island community over the years.

Robert Quayle
Chairman, Steam Packet Co. Ltd
October 2011

There were a number of boat building yards in Douglas and here a fishing vessel the Lady Fry *is under construction on the Tongue. She was launched sideways into the harbour at high water in 1910. (Stan Basnett collection)*

The fine Victoria Pier Building with its imposing clock tower was built in 1890 at the time of the major harbour improvements. The glazed verandah was added later and the building remained in use until 1960 when it was demolished to make way for the present sea terminal. (Stan Basnett collection)

The inner harbour at Douglas seen from the 'double corner'. Before the swing bridge was installed a ferry operated across the harbour. It was customary at Easter to offer trips around the harbour for one penny. (Stan Basnett collection)

Introduction

Following the publication of the *Steam Packet 175* books by Lily Publications both the publisher and I received photographs of Steam Packet vessels from readers who had been prompted by nostalgia to look through their own collections for photographs of Steam Packet vessels.

Subsequently the publisher asked me to compile a pictorial book based on the Steam Packet in the style of *Camera on the Clyde*. The objective was to include work by enthusiasts who had sent material and whose work had not previously been seen along with additional photographs from other established photographers, including myself, embracing wherever possible material not previously seen.

So what is the Steam Packet? Well for those who may not be familiar with shipping in the Irish Sea the Steam Packet is the colloquial name for the Isle of Man Steam Packet Co. Ltd. It was established between 1829 and 1832 by a group of island residents whose principal objective was to improve communication between the Island and Liverpool. The first vessel was launched on 30th June 1830 and named *Mona's Isle*. The Steam Packet was in business.

The home port on the island was Douglas which at the time of the company's formation possessed a tidal harbour with one Pier known as the Tongue in the inner harbour. The outer harbour had the Red Pier that had been built in 1801 which was also tidal. The harbour was protected from easterly gales by the Fort Anne Jetty forming a small outer breakwater.

Problems with landing passengers by small boat at low water led eventually to a low water landing pier being built in the outer harbour and becoming the Queen Victoria Pier. Protection of the outer harbour, which was still exposed to easterly gales, came in the form of successive breakwaters with the Battery pier completed in1876.

The Red Pier was extended to form the King Edward VIII Pier in 1936. The final development of the harbour saw the provision of a new breakwater completed in 1983 and named as the Princess Alexandra Pier giving the outer harbour full protection from easterly gales at last.

Since then the advent of Ro-Ro services has seen the provision of linkspans and marshalling areas being developed in the outer harbour and the inner harbour becoming a half-tide basin and a yacht marina.

Throughout this time the Steam Packet has continued to operate services between the island and north west ports of the UK with seasonal traffic to other destinations within the British Isles.

This book, however, is only going to cover the period from 1930 to the present day. Most but not all of the vessels operated by the company during this period are illustrated in black and white and also in colour along with some of the vessels that have been chartered to cover surveys and freight movement.

The last eighty years has seen progress beyond the imagination of those who commissioned the centenary steamer the ss *Lady of Mann*. When launched she represented the ultimate development of the typical cross-channel steamer. Now with the fast craft *Manannan* the company is still at the forefront of development and is as far away from the original vessels as one can be.

Douglas inner harbour full of steam trawlers during the herring fishery which occurred between July and September. The date is unknown but probably in the 1920s. This part of the harbour between the Tongue and the North Quay has now been partly filled and is a marina. The frontage of the North Quay on the left remains mostly unaltered and the quay partly pedestrianised. (Stan Basnett collection)

This collection of photographs has only been made possible by the generous assistance of the following contributors some of whom are no longer with us but whose contribution through friends and family is gratefully acknowledged.

Doug Allen, Gillian Basnett, Eric Bird, Ian Collard, the late Capt Tom Corteen, Miles Cowsill, the late Henry Clague, Dick Clague, Roy Cressey, Richard Davis, Maurice Dickens, John Hendy, InCat (Australia), Lawrence Macduff, Bryan Kennedy, the late Capt Vernon Kinley, Liverpool Maritime Museum, John Morris, the late Oli Mylrea, Brendan O'Friel, Bruce Peter, Adrian Sweeney, Jenny Williamson, John Williamson and the IoM Steam Packet. Without their photographs this book would not have happened.

The IoM Steam Packet Company had many more vessels than they needed during the winter months so they were laid up at Birkenhead, Barrow and Douglas. Essential maintenance was carried out during this time to ensure that all were available for the intense summer traffic. Two vessels was the maximum that could be accommodated at the Tongue in Douglas. This magnificent photograph shows the **Mona's Queen** *(2) being warped down the harbour to enter service for the summer season. (Richard Davis collection)*

The **Douglas** *is berthed at the company's cargo berth at the Red Pier which dried out at low water. The cargo warehouses are immediately behind the vessel and the large building in the background is the former Imperial Hotel which became the Steam Packet's company offices. (Richard Davis collection)*

French Kier who were the contractors for the new breakwater completed in 1983 encountered some severe winter weather during its construction and placement of the secondary armour. Its completion at last guaranteed protection from easterly gales. (Stan Basnett)

Work in progress on the new Ro-Ro berth on the north side of the King Edward VIII Pier seen from the wheelhouse of the splitter barge **Cork Sand**. *The work was undertaken between 1991 and 1993. (Stan Basnett)*

A photograph of the Lady of Mann *(1) at the Victoria Pier taken by a Mr Taggart for the Douglas Publicity Committee from the Fort Anne Hotel grounds. The* Ben my Chree *(4) is on the other side of the pier. (Stan Basnett collection)*

The Steam Packet Co's vessel Mona *is seen here berthed at Ramsey South Pier at a time when the company ran a mixed cargo and passenger service. She was regularly used and dried out at low water. (Stan Basnett collection)*

A superb evening pre-war photograph of six vessels in the outer harbour at Douglas. It has to have been taken in 1937 as either the Fenella *(3) or the* Tynwald *(4) is berthed at the Victoria Pier and they were nearly all requisitioned by the end of 1938. (Stan Basnett collection)*

A view of Douglas outer harbour with the Lady of Mann *(1) and her older sister* Ben my Chree *(4) berthed at Victoria Pier with the* Victoria *berthed ahead of the 'Lady'. The photograph dates between 1930 and 1932 after which the three almost identical sisters had their hulls painted white. This followed a charter which called for a white ship and the company were so taken with it that they painted their three largest vessels the same. (Stan Basnett collection)*

The company ran excursions between Peel on the west coast of the Island and Belfast and here the Victoria *is berthed at the breakwater to load passengers. (Oli Mylrea/Stan Basnett collection)*

Again a photograph taken at Peel. This time from the shore as the King Orry *(3) passes on a round the island cruise. The company also operated evening cruises and all were well supported. (Oli Mylrea/Stan Basnett collection)*

Two great photographs of **King Orry** *(3). Above: We see her berthed alongside the Landing Stage at Liverpool. (Richard Davis collection). Below: This classic photograph shows her making her approach to Ardrossan harbour with a tricky following wind. (Bruce Peter collection).*

The magnificent triple screw **Viking** *(1) on the measured mile on the Clyde undergoing her acceptance trials on which she averaged 23.53 knots. The ship was built by Armstrong Whitworth of Newcastle-on-Tyne in 1905 and saw service in two World Wars, surviving both to become part of the post-war fleet and survived until 1954. (IoM Steam Packet)*

The twin screw Rushen Castle *formerly the* Duke of Cornwall *was acquired by the company in 1928 from the London and North Western Railway. She was not taken for war service and remained in service with the Steam Packet during the whole of the Second World War and survived into the post-war fleet. (Stan Basnett collection)*

The Snaefell *(4) was built originally as the* Viper *for G & J Burns. The Steam Packet acquired her in 1920 and as with the* Rushen Castle *was funded out of the compensation for war losses in the First World War. The vessel did see service for a short time in World War Two but was returned to the company to maintain its service as a running mate to the* Rushen Castle *and lasted into the post-war fleet. (Liverpool Maritime Museum McRoberts collection)*

The **Manx Maid** *formerly the* **Caesarea** *of the London and South Western Railway Co was another vessel purchased by the company to replace First World War losses and lasted into the post World War Two fleet being eventually scrapped in 1950. (Bruce Peter collection)*

A wonderful photograph of the Mona *(4) at the Red Pier on the Steam Packet cargo berth or as it was sometimes called the office berth. She was formerly the* Hazel *of Laird Line and was another vessel purchased by the company to replace losses. Eventually they were to purchase five having lost seven during the war. (Richard Davis collection)*

Having served as an armed boarding vessel in the First World War the Peel Castle *returned after hostilities and remained in service until 1939. Another former railway steamer she had been the* Duke of York *of the Lancashire and Yorkshire Railway until the Steam Packet purchased her in 1912. (Stan Basnett collection)*

The company enjoyed a near monopoly on what we now know as break bulk cargo traffic. Its first dedicated cargo vessel was the Tyrconnel *(top) seen at Peel East Quay 1911 to 1932. Followed by the* Cushag *(middle) 1920 to 1943 and built for the company by Cammell Laird & Co Ltd and the* Peveril *(2) (bottom) both at Douglas. (Stan Basnett collection)*

The last pre-war cargo vessel to be acquired was the Conister *a single hatch coaster formerly the* Abington *to replace the* Tyrconnel *which was scrapped in 1932. Seen here at night in Douglas inner harbour she was to last until January 1965. (Stan Basnett)*

A very atmospheric photograph showing the Liverpool landing stage which was the gateway to the new world for so many. In this pre-war shot the **Manxman** *(1) is loading passengers prior to sailing and the purser is collecting tickets at the foot of the gangway, something that lasted until the 1980s. (Richard Davis collection)*

After a Board decision to paint the Ben my Chree *(4) white with green boot topping in 1932 for publicity purposes the* Lady of Mann *(1) was similarly treated here she is berthed on the south side of the Victoria Pier with her sister ship berthed on the north side.*
(The late Paul Barton - Stan Basnett collection)

These two photographs show the **Mona's Queen** *(3) to good advantage. They were taken at Ardrossan and the additional deck forward compared with the 'Ben' and the 'Lady' is very evident. The first class dining saloon was located there immediately over the second class dining saloon. The ship and her appointments were much appreciated by passengers. When she was mined at Dunkirk the island was deeply shocked and even three years later I remember it being talked about within the family. For those who were responsible for commanding the ship it was not so popular being called the 'widow maker' on account of the high forepeak catching the wind when approaching and berthing in exposed harbours. (Bruce Peter collection)*

Here the **Fenella** *(2) approaches Ardrossan with a following wind making the final entry to the harbour something of a challenge. (Bruce Peter collection)*

The Tynwald *(4) and* Fenella *(2) were almost identical sister ships and were built by Vickers Armstrong at Barrow. They entered service in 1937 and were both lost during the Second World War. The top of the funnel being parallel to the waterline was their distinguishing feature. Their lasting legacy, however, was their hull form that laid the foundation for the design of the post-war fleet. (Bruce Peter collection)*

Because of the seasonal nature of the business the Steam Packet would lay up all but two of their fleet during the winter months which was adequate to cope with the winter traffic. They were mainly laid up at Barrow and Birkenhead but there would usually be two laid up at Douglas in the inner harbour as in this photograph of the Mona *(4) and* Ramsey Town *at the Tongue. (Richard Davis collection)*

The Ben my Chree *(4) leaving Douglas, well loaded, in company with* King Orry *(3). The height of her funnel is well illustrated and it was eventually shortened after the war to reduce the vessel's tendency to roll. She is carrying her original livery in the photograph which can be dated between 1927 and 1932. (Stan Basnett collection)*

This photograph of Ben my Chree *(4) was taken in August 1965 as she is just about to take the morning sailing from the north side of the King Edward VIII pier. The vessel returned to passenger service after the war having seen service as a troopship and as a Landing Ship Infantry. The shortened funnel is apparent in this photograph. (Eric Bird)*

An atmospheric shot in 1965 of the Ben my Chree *(4) at Liverpool Landing Stage waiting her next turn of duty with not a soul in sight and gently simmering away as boiler room staff make ready. The vessel was fitted with oil firing equipment from new. (The late Henry Clague/Dick Clague collection)*

Another of the 'Ben' going astern out of Douglas in a southerly swell in June 1968 would you believe! The ship is held stern into wind and sea as the fo'c'sle party secure all ropes and the bow rudder before she turns head into sea for Liverpool. (Stan Basnett)

A superbly classic photograph of the Ben my Chree *(4) arriving at Douglas on a beautiful summer evening in August 1965 with the afternoon sailing from Liverpool. Living up to her name as translated from the Manx Gaelic it literally means woman of my heart, or sweetheart.* (Eric Bird)

Above: The 'Ben' is berthed at the King Edward VIII Pier on a summer evening in August 1960 with the rowing boats which you could hire from the promenade being brought into the croak for the night – life really was more leisurely then. Below: a final view of the 'Ben' berthed at the Victoria Pier with the Manxman *(2) berthed on the Battery Pier lay-by berth. (Stan Basnett)*

The Lady of Mann *(1) came back from the war having served as a troopship and then a Landing ship Infantry like her sister and then returned to trooping until March 1946 when she was released returning to Steam Packet service two months later. (Eric Bird)*

This is a fascinating picture from Dick Clague's collection showing the Manx Maid *(1) which also saw war service initially as an armed boarding vessel and survived to return to service with the Steam Packet. She is without its mainmast which was never replaced after the war and here is being towed down the harbour at Douglas by the IoM Harbour Board workboat* Sirdar *and passing the coaster* Avanville *on charter to the Steam Packet at that time.*

The Lady of Mann *(1) leaving Douglas in August 1968 bound for Liverpool with a full complement of passengers. The freedom and popularity of open decks being enjoyed by those on the shelter deck sadly is missing from the modern vessels. (Stan Basnett)*

The Lady of Mann *(1) was a very popular ship during her life and more so in her last decade. The ship was the last representative of the cross-channel steamers employed on the Irish Sea routes and a favourite with enthusiasts. The photograph shows her leaving Ardrossan on 14th August 1971. (Lawrence Macduff)*

Three photographs of Lady of Mann *(1) at Ramsey which was a regular call up until the early 70s with ships of the company sailing to Ardrossan and occasionally Belfast. The Queen's Pier was built as a low water landing facility as the harbour dries at low water. (Stan Basnett)*

These three photographs should give those who are too young to have travelled on her an idea of what the 'Lady' was like. In the dining room the meals were silver service and waited on by a steward and the lounges had comfortable settees and the ladies still had an exclusive lounge. The officers also ate in the dining room, their only concession being a reserved table. (Top photo Stan Basnett. Lower photos Lawrence Macduff)

The Victoria *also survived her war service first as one of the remaining vessels maintaining the Liverpool passenger service until an altercation with a mine in the Mersey in 1940. After repair she undertook various duties ending up trooping until being released in 1947. She lasted in service until 1956 being employed only in the summer months. This superb view from the Richard Davis collection shows her arriving at the Liverpool Landing Stage.*

The Viking *seen arriving at the Victoria Pier on a tranquil summer evening was a real survivor having seen service in two World Wars and lasting with the Company until the end of the 1954 season. The traveller could enjoy the freedom of the open decks, the warmth of the funnels on a cold day and the smuts in your eye! (Stan Basnett collection)*

Now we come to the new post-war fleet which started with the building of King Orry *(4) by Cammell Laird & Co Ltd at Birkenhead. She entered service with the Company in 1946 and it was immediately apparent that her pedigree lay with pre-war* Fenella *and* Tynwald *and the proven hull form evolved by experience in the Irish Sea. Here she is seen arriving at Douglas. (Stan Basnett)*

The name King Orry comes from the first Norse King of Mann and it was appropriate that the ship was the first of a new class of vessel for the Company. Here King Orry *(4) glides into the harbour at Douglas approaching the berth on the north side of the King Edward VIII Pier. The engineers in anticipation of the call for 'full astern' have bled some steam onto one of the turbines. (Stan Basnett)*

The King Orry *(4) made her final voyage at the end of the 1975 season and was sold for breaking. After lying for three years at Glasson Dock she was eventually towed to Kent and broken up at Strood on the Medway. (John Hendy)*

The King Orry *(4) on winter service backs out of Douglas in an easterly gale. She originally had a cravat on the funnel but it was removed early in her life. (Stan Basnett)*

In this photograph she is seen approaching the Victoria Pier for the end berth on the north side and going full astern. As she loses forward motion the wind will set her down on the pier as she comes to a stop. (Stan Basnett)

The summer season doesn't always imply good weather particularly in August when fog is often a problem and particularly in September when the autumnal equinox hands out guaranteed gales. King Orry *(4) is seen arriving in such conditions at Douglas on the tail of a southerly gale. Note the bow rudder. (Stan Basnett)*

The next ship in the new post-war fleet was the Mona's Queen *(4) and she entered service the same week as* King Orry *(4). Both ships were built at Birkenhead and carried consecutive yard numbers. The photograph shows her in the Mersey about to make a turn and approach the Landing Stage. (Adrian Sweeney collection)*

The first five of the post-war builds were almost identical sisters the first two having only one cutaway on the starboard side of the boat deck to facilitate loading cars at the King Edward VIII Pier. All subsequent sister ships had cutaways each side and detail differences in window layouts. In this photograph the Mona's Queen *(4) is seen at Ardrossan. (Bruce Peter collection)*

Although the Mona's Queen *(4) was the first disposal from the fleet she did outlast her sisters sailing in Greek waters until being broken up at Perama in 1981. In this photograph she is seen leaving Dublin bound for Douglas. (Adrian Sweeney collection)*

The next to arrive was the Tynwald *(5) seen here berthed on the north side of the King Edward VIII Pier and about to leave on Monday 2nd August 1971, three blasts on the whistle indicating her intention to all. The rowing boats known affectionately as the 'rowies' have not left the harbour as the visitors haven't finished breakfast! (Eric Bird)*

The Tynwald *(5) arriving at Douglas photographed from the end of the Battery Pier, which is still accessible but the new breakwater projects further seaward and the angle of approach has changed the perspective and meaning it is no longer such a good place to photograph shipping arriving at the port. (Stan Basnett)*

The company policy from the outset was to name most of their vessels with Manx connections and Tynwald is the name of the Manx Parliament. Here the Tynwald *(5) is berthed at the Victoria Pier waiting for departure with retuning day trippers judging by the flags. (Eric Bird)*

This quite reflective view of the Tynwald *(5) leaving Douglas was shot in the winter of 1964/5 and belies the fact that it was one of the island's worst winters for snow! (Eric Bird)*

The fourth ship to enter the post-war fleet in 1948 was the **Snaefell** *(5) and she was the first with four windows to the officer's accommodation below the bridge, which was a handy distinguishing feature. She is named after the island's highest mountain and in the top picture she is seen in July 1977 approaching Ardrossan. In the lower picture she is approaching Douglas in a south-easterly blow with a following wind and swell which will require all the master's skill when entering the harbour. Note the Chief Officer climbing down the ratlines from the bridge to take his position on the f'o'c'sle. (Lawrence Macduff/Stan Basnett)*

Peel was used as the diversionary port for Douglas when Douglas was untenable due to easterly gales and here Mona's Isle *(5), the last of the true five sisters has just arrived and a bus awaits the passengers who will be taken by road to Douglas to complete their journey. The photo was taken in February 1966, the one bus is an indication that it was winter and that there were few passengers. (Stan Basnett)*

The Mona's Isle *(5) arrives at Douglas in August 1968 with another day trip indicated by the flags flying from the foremast. The name in this case is self explanatory with Mona being an alternative name for the island. (Eric Bird)*

A fine view of the ship this time as she leaves Douglas. She entered service in 1951 and went to the breakers in 1980. (John Morris)

Another photograph by John Morris of the Mona's Isle *(5) at Llandudno. All sailings to and from the Welsh port were day trips and it was a tradition with the company that they should be dressed. I often wondered if the code flags actually spelt something – perhaps it was best not to find out! In the background the* St Trillo *is seen having left ahead of her arrival.*

Here are three photos of **Snaefell** *(5) at two different locations. Top picture shows Ardrossan harbour from the bridge. (The late Capt. Tom Corteen). The lower pictures show her arriving at Ramsey Queens Pier from Ardrossan in the evening sunshine in August 1966 and leaving the Pier to continue her sailing to Douglas. The* **Snaefell** *(5) and the* **Mona's Isle** *(5) were the last two of the five sisters to remain in service after 1975, the* **Mona's Isle** *(5) being the last going for scrap in 1980 after thirty years service with the Company. (Eric Bird)*

This photograph of **Snaefell** *(5) has been published before but in black and white. Here it is in colour although there isn't much difference! It was late in the afternoon towards the end of January 1970 and snowing driven by a biting easterly wind. This was the second attempt, the first being aborted in the middle of a whiteout. These ships didn't have the advantage of bow thrust or bridge control of the propellers and Peel was a difficult entry, as we shall see later. The two lower winter photographs of her arriving at Douglas were also something of a challenge. It does tend to give the publisher problems as he prefers the sun to shine on every photograph! (Stan Basnett)*

By contrast here is a beautiful photograph of Mona's Isle *(5) with a departure from Douglas taken in the actinic light of evening. Unfortunately this location is no longer available to us due to the security regulations in place around the harbour. (John Morris)*

Photography does have its ups and downs and to prove a point that the sun doesn't always shine in the summer here are two more photographs of **Mona's Isle** *(5) heading out of Douglas on 12th June 1973 bound for Llandudno in a southerly swell left over from an earlier south westerly gale. (Stan Basnett)*

The Mona's Isle *(5) being the last of the five sisters did get photographed more than the others because of her longevity so here are two from my library that show the two extremes in her last years.*

In this photograph John Morris has captured the essence of those glorious days in the 60s and early 70s when scenes like this could be captured particularly at weekends when there were numerous sailings both outward and inward from Scotland, Ireland and England and the island still had a holiday industry albeit a shadow of pre-war activity. The Mona's Isle *(5) is seen backing out of Douglas as the* Snaefell *(5) having completed her turn is already underway for Liverpool. (John Morris)*

Now we come to the sixth post-war build which is almost but not quite a sister to the others. The Manxman *(2) entered service in 1955 also built by Cammell Laird & Co Ltd but she (I do have problems with the convention that requires a ship to be female when its name is distinctly male!) was fitted with the latest Pametrada turbines and had her lifeboats slung on Wallin davits leaving the boat deck clear of obstruction. Here she is seen passing under the Erskine Bridge on the Clyde on 3rd May 1977 having been docked for survey. (Lawrence Macduff)*

The Manxman *(2) in Govan in 1980 where on occasion company vessels were docked for survey or lay-up as necessary but at this period Birkenhead West Float was still the preferred option. (Lawrence Macduff)*

Above: It is hard now, with the paranoia of Health and Safety legislation, to remember the freedom we enjoyed that is typified by this photograph taken on the fo'c'sle as the Manxman *(2) approaches Llandudno. The chief officer is in charge and no doubt will move people when the ship is berthing. (John Hendy)*

Left: The Manxman *(2) became the last of the conventional ferries being sold by the company in 1982. The picture below shows her under way passing Douglas Head. (John Hendy)*

The **Manxman** *(2) leaves Douglas with her last sailing to Llandudno dressed overall for the occasion accompanied by Laxey Towing Co's tug* **Salisbury**. *(Stan Basnett)*

Before the advent of Ro-Ro and the clear hatch conversion of **Peveril** *(3) double deck buses were carried across the forepeak of certain passenger vessels that had removable railings for the purpose and* **Manxman** *(2) was one. (Stan Basnett)*

It was normal practice for company vessels to berth bow in at Douglas and leave astern before the advent of bow thrusters. Very occasionally ships would be warped around the head of the pier to leave bow first. The **Manxman** *(2) is about to leave having been turned at the Edward VIII Pier in 1966. (Stan Basnett)*

The Manxman *(2) became the last of the conventional ferries being sold by the company in 1982. Capt. Peter Corrin (top left) was her last popular master and held with fond affection by many enthusiasts. (Top right) The Marconi Radio Operator tucked away on the* Manxman. *(Above) The dining room whilst not quite as grand as the old* Lady of Mann *still had waiter service, tablecloths, silver service and proper chairs! (John Hendy)*

Southerly swells off the harbour entrance and easterly gales always made entry to Douglas difficult. The winter berth was always the south side of the King Edward VIII Pier but here there was often a sting in the tail. It was essential to get the bow in to the pier first as the stern could be brought in with the engines against a bow spring. If there was a strong run of fresh water running down the harbour and the tide was full the bow would fetch up against the Fort Anne Jetty as we see Manxman *(2) in such a predicament on 19th April 1965. (Stan Basnett)*

Here is a much calmer situation as the Manxman *(2) pulls away from the berthing head at Ramsey Queens Pier on her way to Belfast on the 4th August 1970 having embarked two passengers. The advent of the car ferries led to an end to this practice although they did call occasionally up to the time the pier closed to shipping. (Stan Basnett)*

Another fine photograph by Eric Bird of the Manxman *(2) taken in 1969 as she leaves Douglas with a full complement of happy visitors at the end of their holiday.*

The Manxman *(2) makes a smart departure from Douglas at a time when her future was uncertain with the threat of competition imminent. The writing was on the wall as a linkspan and approach road were to be built at Douglas and Manx Line was to introduce a Ro-Ro service between Heysham and Douglas. (John Morris)*

Everything was happening at once for the Company not only the threat of competition but also rumblings that a takeover might happen – grim days indeed. The Manxman *(2) lies at the Victoria Pier on 12th July 1978 and Carmet Towing's* Dunheron *is at the Edward Pier preparing to tow away contractors' equipment prior to the arrival of the new linkspan. (Stan Basnett)*

The **Manxman** *(2) was sold in 1982 to Marda (Squash) Ltd for conversion into a sports complex at Preston and sailed to her new location under her own steam. The venture did not succeed and she was subsequently sold for further conversion as a night club. In this photograph she is berthed at Preston with her future uncertain. (Maurice Dickens)*

The **King Orry** *(4) aground in the Lune Estuary in 1976 having been blown off the quay at Glasson Dock where she was to be broken up. Eventually it was scrapped in Kent as we saw earlier. (Stan Basnett)*

The **Manxman** *(2) is another ship that refuses to go quietly and the vessel is seen here in a very sad state in Pallion Dock Gateshead in 2010 awaiting her fate. (Adrian Sweeney)*

The **Conister** *(1) was one of the pre-war cargo vessels that survived. Built in 1921 as the* **Abington** *and purchased by the Company in 1932 she gave 33 years service to the company and survived as the last single hatch steam coaster trading in the Irish Sea. (Stan Basnett)*

The Conister *(1) was towed away from Douglas on 26th January 1965 by Steel & Bennie's tug* Campaigner *for breaking at Dalmuir. (Stan Basnett)*

The Fenella *(3) was an important step for the Company. She was the first new build cargo ship after the war and was launched in 1951 at the Ailsa Shipbuilding Co. Ltd at Troon. She was also the first motor ship breaking a long tradition with steam. She was sold for further trading in 1973. (Stan Basnett)*

This shot of the **Fenella** *(3) leaving Douglas was taken from the Victoria Pier now no longer accessible for port security reasons. The late John Nicholson RA and marine artist was an early member of the local branch of the World Ship Society and it was he who brought the use of actinic light to the notice of those of us who were into photography. The sun lights the face of the subject when low in the sky avoiding deep shadows such as occurs at midday. (Stan Basnett)*

The Steam Packet continued trading in break bulk cargo and maintained services between Douglas, Ramsey and Coburg dock in Liverpool. They had a warehouse at Ramsey usually the domain of the **Conister** *(1) but here* **Fenella** *(3) is on a rare visit to Ramsey. (Stan Basnett)*

The cargo services were maintained as a liner service all year round which often resulted in opportunities for some spectacular photographs of the cargo vessels arriving in bad weather. (Stan Basnett)

In 1962 the Company took delivery of its second motor vessel also built at Troon and named her **Peveril** *(3). In the top picture the vessel is at the company's cargo berth dressed overall on the occasion of her arrival at Douglas for the first time. She was fitted with two modern derrick cranes each with a capacity of ten tons for self discharge. In the lower picture she is leaving the steam crane berth on the Battery Pier having discharged a heavy load. (Stan Basnett)*

The **Peveril** *(3) continued to operate in this form for nine years but the company could no longer continue with break bulk cargo. Their hand was forced by competition from another local company operating out of Castletown that was handling container traffic. The result was that she was converted to a cellular cargo vessel in 1972 and shore handling equipment installed. The lower right picture shows her in her later guise. She was sold for further service in 1981. (Stan Basnett)*

In 1964 the Company took delivery of a third post-war cargo vessel and once again she was a motor vessel and from the Ailsa yard in Troon. She was designed as a replacement for Conister *(1) principally for use on the Ramsey/Liverpool run and they named her* Ramsey *in acknowledgement of this. The prospective captains of the passenger ships cut their teeth on the cargo vessels and you can see why they became very aware of the nature of the sea states around the harbour approaches as the* Ramsey *enters Douglas on a winter's day. (Stan Basnett)*

Here the Ramsey *leaves her home port on 6th July 1966 and is passing the ICI Mond division coaster* Lady Roslin *discharging supplies of explosives for local quarries. (Stan Basnett)*

This photograph shows the Ramsey *lifting on one of those swells that I have mentioned several times as she leaves Douglas. You could guarantee their presence after a southerly gale had blown for a day or two as the fetch would run unhindered from the St George's Channel and the presence of shelving rocks from St Mary's Isle in the bay would cause these lumps across the harbour entrance. Alas no more, as dredging for the new approach channel removed them and the harbour entrance is now further out and inaccessible. (Stan Basnett)*

The Manx Maid *(2) was the first of a new breed of car ferry commissioned by the Company. Built at Cammell Laird & Co Ltd she retained the proven hull form of the post-war sisters below the waterline. She was very much a pioneer being built with integrated car ramps to enable side loading of cars without either stern or bow loading ramps. The Company came in for a lot of criticism over this but it had to design for the ports it served, all of which had no Ro-Ro facilities. The design was successful and it led to four such ferries being built. (Stan Basnett)*

The **Manx Maid** *(2) was retro fitted with a bow thrust unit following the success of those fitted from new to the* **Mona's Queen** *(5). This allowed her to turn in the outer harbour and leave bow first and saving almost quarter of an hour on the journey time with no need to turn and secure the bow rudder. She is seen sporting one of several logos that were tried as a marketing ploy. (Stan Basnett)*

The **Manx Maid** *(2) leaves Douglas in the winter of 1962/3 on a beautiful crisp clear morning such as would happen with a north westerly wind direction. The* **Fenella** *(2) waits for clearance to enter having had a stormy overnight crossing. (Stan Basnett)*

The **Manx Maid** *(2) having been diverted to Peel due to easterly gales departs for Liverpool from Peel. Usually if the gale abated overnight the ship would be repositioned to Douglas for the following morning sailing. Here the storm is still blowing from the east. (Stan Basnett)*

Two more photographs of Manx Maid *(2) presenting almost contradictory stories. (Top picture) she is seen arriving at Peel in April 1966 to discharge passengers and cars. She will have been diverted because of conditions at Douglas but here on the other side of the Island conditions seem almost deceptively idyllic. The lower photograph shows her leaving Douglas in anything but idyllic conditions when you would expect her to be at Peel. It is almost certain that it has freshened overnight from the south east guaranteeing an interesting crossing! (Eric Bird/Stan Basnett)*

The next side loader to arrive was the Ben my Chree *(5) in 1966 also having been built at Birkenhead. Like the* Manx Maid *(2) she was a twin-screw steam turbine ship with a service speed of 21.5 knots, they had a lot of tradition built into their hull design and were exceptional vessels. Here she is seen surfing in to Douglas on those swells I mentioned earlier. (Stan Basnett)*

Here are the first two car ferries together and you can compare the slight differences between them. The **Manx Maid** *(2) is in the upper picture and the 'Ben' in the lower. I am not sadistic at all I just like photographing ships in stormy weather! (Stan Basnett)*

The photograph (above) was taken in the early evening with Ben my Chree *(5) berthed on the south side of the King Edward VIII Pier in company with three other company vessels. The* Lady of Mann *(1) can be seen loading day trippers back to Llandudno. (John Morris) Both of these car ferries were fitted with stabilisers which of course made for a more comfortable crossing in rough weather but they had to be retracted for entry into harbour and in Douglas it coincided with the shallowing water giving passengers a reminder of the state of the sea as the 'Ben' (right) makes a lively approach to Douglas. (Stan Basnett)*

The Ben my Chree *(5), which literally translates as a woman of my heart or colloquially 'sweetheart', sits at Ardrossan on 29th June 1980 with the blue peter at the fore ready to load for her departure to Douglas. (Lawrence Macduff)*

The Ben my Chree *(5) sits in the evening sun at the south side of the King Edward VIII Pier. Just ahead of the bow there is a white diamond painted on the wall that marks the presence of the harbour bar from which point the harbour dries at low water. On the seaward side the berth has sufficient water for the ferries to berth at low water. It was yet another hazard when approaching the berth on a falling tide. (Maurice Dickens)*

The Ben my Chree *(5) like her sister ship was retro fitted with a bow thruster but until then passengers were given an unpleasant few minutes while turning in lumpy weather before getting under way. (Stan Basnett)*

The 'Ben' on the north side of the Edward Pier and in the background the new Steam Packet linkspan can be seen – change was coming. Initially the company operated a freight only Ro-Ro service. (Stan Basnett)

Here is an interesting sequence illustrating the fact that entry to Peel in an easterly wind was also a challenge. The conventional entry with the traditional ships was to approach the end of the breakwater at a slight angle and stop with the stern just overlapping. The wind would then carry the vessel's stern onto the pier and swing the bow onto the berth checking with engines and anchor as necessary. Here the Ben my Chree *(5) is approaching straight on and using her bow thrust unit to push the bow in. Unfortunately the wind has got behind the stern and pushed her onto the sand bar which is a further hazard. With little water under her, berthing was difficult but eventually successful. (Stan Basnett)*

A stern view of the **Ben my Chree** *(5) leaving Douglas showing the beautiful lines of these ferries. I know that beauty is in the eye of the beholder but the sheer and hull form seem to me anyway far more attractive than the present generation of floating boxes. Is it romanticism that makes an enthusiast? (Stan Basnett)*

Now to the next generation of car ferries and the introduction of the first passenger motor vessels. First a comparison between the **Ben my Chree** *(5) at Heysham in the photograph above and in the lower photograph the* **Mona's Queen** *(5) at Plymouth on charter to La Poste in support of their entry at the start of a Round the World yacht race. (John Hendy)*

Two contrasting photographs of the **Mona's Queen** *(5) well illustrate that the Isle of Man is an island and subject to extremes of weather. It was customary to place the newer vessels on the winter service. A winter departure (above) shows her butting into an easterly to turn as the strength of wind prohibited turning in the outer harbour, she was the first to be fitted with a bow thruster from new. By way of a contrast the view (left) was taken on a Round the Island trip turning under Bradda Head within Port Erin Bay. The new breed were exceptionally manoeuvrable having bridge control of variable pitch propellers. (Stan Basnett)*

The **Mona's Queen** *(5) was built by Ailsa Shipbuilding Co. Ltd., Troon and was launched in 1972. She was to give the company 23 years service and like all the car ferries was employed all year round initially running with one of the earlier car ferries on the Liverpool route discharging cars at the landing stage. (Stan Basnett)*

Here is another illustration of the difficulties that could be encountered when entering Douglas in a south easterly gale. The **Mona's Queen** *(5) makes her approach to Douglas on 9th November 1972 and speed has to be kept up to maintain steerage in the conditions. One of those shelving swells hits her as the harbour is entered knocking her off her line of approach for the south side of the King Edward VIII Pier...........*

..... but it is high tide and there is a lot of fresh water running down the harbour from the river Douglas which compounds the situation. Suddenly she is stemming the pier and full astern on the combinators avoids a serious incident.

Now she is in the middle of the outer harbour with the wind taking control and only skilful use of the engines and bow thrust enables control to be regained. She successfully berthed at the Victoria Pier. (Stan Basnett)

Being an islander you are more aware of the weather and the state of the sea. This would present opportunities for spectacular photographs but of course misery for passengers. Here **Mona's Queen** *(5) is making her run across Douglas bay to enter the harbour. (Stan Basnett)*

The two photographs of **Mona's Queen** *(5) on this page further illustrate the conditions just off the harbour entrance at Douglas after a prolonged southerly gale has abated guaranteeing an uncomfortable start to the journey. In the top photograph she is taking the swell on the beam and the stabiliser slot is clear of the water giving a clear indication of just how far over she is rolling. In the photograph below the turn has been completed and she is getting under way but still in the comparatively shallow water off the harbour as she climbs out of the swell. (Stan Basnett)*

Although the sea conditions don't appear nearly so bad in these two photographs the underlying swell is still there as can be seen in these two photographs of Mona's Queen *(5) leaving Douglas. (Stan Basnett)*

The Mona's Queen *(5) was joined by* Lady of Mann *(2) in 1975, an almost identical sister ship, and here both are in winter lay-up in Birkenhead. The* Mona's Queen *(5) was sold in 1995 for further service in the Philippines. (Maurice Dickens)*

The **Mona's Queen** *(5) above made her final voyage with the Steam Packet at the end of the 1990 summer season and was laid up at Birkenhead and offered for sale. It was to be five years before a buyer was found. She did enter service with MBS Lines and was renamed* **Mary the Queen** *and is seen in the photograph left berthed at Manilla. (Maurice Dickens/Ian Collard)*

Now that the Steam Packet was offering a fully containerised Lo-Lo service a running mate was required for the Peveril *(3) to handle the volume of traffic. The* Spaniel *was initially chartered from Coast Lines in July 1973 and was purchased in November the same year and renamed* Conister *(2). She is seen in the top photograph leaving the cargo berth where a 25-ton capacity Butters derrick crane had been installed. The photograph below shows the vessel in dry dock at Govan in company with the paddle steamer* Waverley *in October 1978. (Stan Basnett/Lawrence Macduff)*

Fleetwood sailings were still a regular destination in the seasonal timetable. Here the Lady of Mann *(2) is berthed at Fleetwood. (Maurice Dickens)*

The company experimented with different corporate liveries applied to the hull of their vessels, not all of which proved popular, this is one carried by the 'Lady' as she butts into that swell again leaving for Dublin. (Stan Basnett)

Dick Clague was fortunate enough to get this interesting photograph of the Lady of Mann *(2) in dry dock for survey at Birkenhead.*

The Lady of Mann *(2) was the second passenger motor vessel to be built for the company and like her sister ship was built at the Ailsa Shipbuilding Co., Ltd at Troon. She was the fourth and last of the side loading car ferries and was fitted with 12-cylinder engines which were more powerful than the* Mona's Queen *(5). This gave her a useful service speed of 22 knots which made her popular on the Liverpool and Ardrossan routes. The photograph above shows her approaching Ardrossan and the one on the left is a fine photograph of her leaving Ardrossan. (Lawrence Macduff)*

The Lady of Mann *(2) was altered in 1989 to increase her car carrying capacity and these photographs show the difference to the profile as a result, the additional car space being located above the car deck. She is photographed at Whitehaven on one of a number of pre-season day trips operated by the Company. (Bryan Kennedy)*

The Lady of Mann *(2) is seen here just about to leave the Liverpool Landing Stage with a full complement on board with cars parked up the ramps. The logo was not the final one carried by the vessel but it was generally thought to suit her lines best. (Brendan O'Friel)*

The Lady of Mann *(2) became the last vessel operated by the company running pre-season day trips to and from ports such as Llandudno, Fleetwood, Whitehaven and Warrenpoint. They were well supported and proved extremely popular. Here she is leaving Llandudno under the shadow of the Great Orme returning day trippers to Douglas having celebrated one hundred years of Steam Packet vessels sailing to the town. (Brendan O'Friel)*

The 'Lady' made a number of these trips almost as her swan song and were well supported as enthusiasts realised that each season may be her last. The trip that many consider as the epic was a two-day trip to Troon on 20th and 21st May 2005 when she returned to her roots, where she had been built, thirty years after her launch. (John Williamson)

In this view looking back at the 'Lady' berthed at the breakwater shows clearly how cross-channel ferries have outgrown many of the ports they once served. (Jenny Williamson)

I mentioned earlier that the Company was criticised by some that it had not moved into Ro-Ro early enough. Troon is a classic example of a port with restricted draught and berthing facilities which was the reason why the Company developed the unconventional side-loading hull design. (John Williamson)

Among the farewell trips made by the Lady of Mann *(2) was one to Barrow on 25th May 2005. Barrow was once a familiar place for company vessels and the long day trip included an optional coach trip to the Lake District. The photograph on the left shows the pilot launch approaching the 'Lady' as she enters the Walney Channel under the watchful eye of three of the contributors to this book! In the photograph above she is passing Walney Island in more sheltered water preparatory to entering the dock system. (Stan Basnett/Bryan Kennedy)*

After a long day ashore and a trip to the Lake District the Lady of Mann *(2) awaits the return of the passengers before leaving for Douglas. (Stan Basnett)*

The **Lady of Mann** *(2) was retained longer than expected to cover winter schedules when fastcraft sailings were disrupted by weather and then used for the additional traffic for the TT Motorcycle races. The vessel was surplus to requirements for the rest of the summer season and the Company was fortunate to find charter work for her. Since 1995 she had seen service in the Azorian Archipelago. In the photograph above she is departing from Pico Island that is dominated by its extinct volcano from which the island gets its name. In the photograph left the 'Lady' is seen departing from Hosta on the island of Faial. (Bryan Kennedy)*

Yet another of the day trips this time with the Lady of Mann *(2) at Fleetwood on 22nd May 2005 about to depart for Douglas. The* Stena Leader *is on the Ro-Ro berth in the background. The usual party of enthusiasts are there to capture the moment. (Jenny Williamson)*

This stunning photograph taken mid passage from the port wing of the bridge, before security became an issue, captures the magic of the Lady of Mann *(2) as we all like to remember her. (Maurice Dickens)*

The 'Lady' was sold for further service to Greek operators SAOS Ferries and extensively altered around the stern to allow the carriage of commercial vehicles on their routes between the Greek Islands. Renamed the Panagia Soumela *she is seen here at the port of Agios Kirikos on the island of Ikaria in April 2008. (Bryan Kennedy)*

Faced with the loss of freight traffic and increasing competition from rival company Manx Line the Steam Packet had no alternative other than to install their own linkspan and charter a vessel to compete. Conditions imposed by the harbour authority meant that the linkspan had to be capable of being moved as proposed improvements to Douglas outer harbour took place. The facility was initially positioned on the south side of the King Edward VIII pier and the NF Jaguar *was chartered in November 1981, being purchased in 1993 and renamed the* Peveril *(4). (Stan Basnett)*

The Steam Packet had maintained an essential link for the carriage of freight to the island for 180 years in the face of competition even as recently as 2010. The Island depends on this link for the daily import of essential goods and it has been maintained in all weathers with containerised traffic on Peveril *(3) above and* Conister *(2) below and prior to that with break bulk cargo vessels. Now all of that traffic is carried to the island by the Ro-Ro service. (Stan Basnett)*

In this photograph taken in July 1981. The Manx Viking *now in Sealink colours, and with the weight of Sea Containers behind the operation, is on the Manx Line linkspan at the Victoria Pier. The different nature of the Steam Packet linkspan sitting on the harbour bed on the south side of the King Edward VIII pier can be clearly seen as* NF Jaguar *is undertaking berthing trials prior to commencing charter. (Stan Basnett)*

The two lower photographs are taken from the control cabin of the Steam Packet linkspan in August 1981 and shows the NF Jaguar *leaving Douglas with a full load and the competition for freight traffic at its height. Was a merger in sight? (Stan Basnett)*

The inevitable merger took place between Sealink/Manx Line and the Steam Packet in February 1985 and would continue to trade as the Steam Packet but with the resources of Sea Containers available to it. The first indication of what this would mean saw the arrival of the **Hoverspeed Great Britain**, *Incat hull No. 025, to the island to show her potential to politicians and others. The photograph of* **Peveril** *(4) now in Steam Packet livery was taken from the fast craft as she made a short trip to Ramsey and back. (Stan Basnett)*

The **Peveril** *(4) is seen here just leaving her berth and about to depart from Douglas for Heysham. (Maurice Dickens)*

The **Peveril** *(4) arrives at Douglas for the last time and turns in the croak before dropping down onto her berth in July 1998. (Miles Cowsill)*

Another look at some of the freight vessels which have been chartered by the Steam Packet. With the company operating their Ro-Ro service out of Heysham it is not surprising that we saw freighters from Seatruck Ferries on the Heysham/Douglas run. The Moondance *was on charter during June 2006 to clear a freight backlog due to the TT festival. (Stan Basnett)*

The identical sister ship to the Moondance *was the* Riverdance *and she was chartered in June 2007 for the same reason. Here she turns in the croak to drop down onto the Victoria Pier linkspan with the* Ben my Chree *(6) occupying the main linkspan on the Edward VIII Pier. (Stan Basnett)*

The Daunt Rock *was chartered to cover the annual survey and dry docking of Peveril (4) during September 1979. (Stan Basnett)*

During 1984 the Steam Packet were looking for a suitable second hand vessel to operate a ro-pax service between Douglas and Heysham and settled in October for the purchase of the former Free Enterprise III *which had been operating as the* Tamira *of the Mira Shipping Line and was lying at Malta for sale. The photograph shows her carrying her new name and in Steam Packet colours leaving Valetta harbour in Malta for the UK where a number of alterations were undertaken prior to the vessel entering service in April 1985 as the* Mona's Isle *(6). (The late Capt. Vernon Kinley)*

The Mona's Isle *(6) entered service on 5th April 1985, which was co-incident with the merger of Manx Line with the Steam Packet. The most obvious alteration was a rather ugly additional lounge added on the boat deck aft. However more significant alterations internally were to lead to her being sold for further service in the Middle East by the end of the year. These two photographs are both taken off Douglas Head of the ship underway and approaching Douglas harbour. (Stan Basnett)*

The Mona's Isle *(6) was a popular ship and here she is entering Douglas harbour with a full complement of passengers many of whom are enjoying the open deck forward which was always popular and reminiscent of earlier Steam Packet boats. It was a clue to her age as she had been built in 1966 when this style was still in vogue. (Stan Basnett)*

Here she approaches Douglas in a summer gale (above left) maintaining her schedule and operating on the old Steam Packet linkspan on the south side of the King Edward VIII Pier. Towards the end of the season continuing problems with the bow thrust unit needed tug assistance from Laxey Towing Co's tug Salisbury*. It was a great pity that* Mona's Isle *(6) didn't realise her full potential – she was too old and too late! (Stan Basnett)*

The Mona's Isle *(6) leaves Douglas with an afternoon sailing almost at the end of her time with the Company having been assisted off the berth by the tug* Salisbury*. She is resplendent in her Steam Packet Colours showing off the lines of the former Townsend Car Ferries to great effect. (Stan Basnett)*

She was sold to Sadaka Shipping in 1986 for further service in the Middle-East and here she is in yet another livery as the Al Fahad*. The ship was wrecked in 2004, near Jeddah, Saudi Arabia. (Ferry Publications Library)*

The **Manx Viking** *was the flagship of the rival company Manx Line and is seen here turning in the outer harbour at Douglas in July 1978 shortly after entering service to establish the island's first Ro-Ro service. (Gillian Basnett)*

By the end of 1978 Sealink had obtained a controlling interest in Manx Line and the **Manx Viking** *ultimately carried the smart Sealink livery and with the resource of Sealink behind the company we were to see many other Sealink vessels on the Isle of Man routes. (Stan Basnett)*

The **Manx Viking** *was the former* **Monte Castillo** *of the Aznar Line and her introduction to the island was to revolutionise freight handling forever. This tranquil photograph of an evening arrival from Heysham belies the underlying turmoil as the ship was plagued with financial and mechanical problems from the outset but despite these and other problems with their linkspan Manx Line eventually established a reliable service thanks to the involvement of Sealink. (Stan Basnett)*

When the **Manx Viking** *first entered service she carried loading gantries that made her somewhat tender. These were removed by Manx Line in 1978 in an effort to improve her sea keeping qualities. After the merger with Sealink more improvements were made and in 1981 during annual survey at Holyhead the opportunity was taken to change her livery and place the island's three-legged emblem on the funnels. Contrast this livery above and on the previous page with the two photographs below showing her in the original livery. The* **Manx Viking** *became part of the Steam Packet Fleet from the time of the merger of the Steam Packet with Sealink Manx Line in 1985. (Stan Basnett)*

Now the strength of the involvement of Sea Containers in the Steam Packet operation became apparent when the former* Antrim Princess *was placed on the Douglas/Heysham route in October 1985 to replace the* Mona's Isle *(6). She was renamed* Tynwald *(6) and served the company until 1990. (Stan Basnett)

Here we see the Tynwald *(6) resplendent in full Steam Packet livery having just arrived from Heysham and commencing her turn in the outer harbour to back down onto the Victoria Pier linkspan. (Stan Basnett)*

The Steam Packet now had the use of two linkspans at Douglas both of which were now owned by the company. The Tynwald *(6) is berthed on the King Edward VIII Pier linkspan and the p.s.* Waverley *can just be seen on the north side of the pier. (Stan Basnett)*

An evening arrival of the Tynwald *(6) towards the end of 1989 it was to be her last full year of operation and she was sold the following year for operation in Italian waters. (Stan Basnett)*

The Steam Packet now had to set about the task of finding a suitable replacement for the Tynwald *(6). On 9th January 1990 Sealink's* Channel Entente *(formerly the* St Eloi*) arrived at Douglas for berthing trials. She presented a magnificent sight as she entered Douglas shortly after the departure of the morning sailing to Heysham. In the lower photograph the power and manoeuvrability of the vessel was immediately apparent. Berthing trials were successful on both linkspans. (Stan Basnett)*

She was purchased by the Steam Packet and entered service on 14th February 1990 sailing without a name change until December when she became King Orry *(5) at a naming ceremony held on board on 8th December 1990 at Douglas. The photograph below shows her arriving at Heysham capturing the mood of a winter arrival perfectly and above departing from Douglas resplendent in her white livery, and finally a view of her arriving at Liverpool. (Maurice Dickens)*

A superb photograph of King Orry *(5) in Wright and Beyer's Bidston dry dock for annual survey on 8th February 1997. (Dick Clague)*

There was no doubt that the white hull of the King Orry *(5) gave her a stunning presence as we see in this photograph of a late afternoon arrival at Douglas with* Claymore *berthed at the Victoria Pier. (Miles Cowsill)*

In this photograph of the King Orry *(5) entering the harbour we can see an alteration that was made later in the year when a door was cut in the starboard side of the hull to allow side loading of cars and vans at Liverpool Landing Stage. (Miles Cowsill)*

Here is the door in action at Liverpool. It is an interesting throw back to the time that the company was a pioneer in side loading car ferries. There is no doubt that it increased the versatility of the ship allowing her to operate as a car ferry from Liverpool. (Miles Cowsill)

Another stunning photograph of King Orry *(5) as she enters Douglas with the afternoon sailing from Heysham. To many this was seen as the best livery carried by Steam Packet vessels. (Miles Cowsill)*

Our band of enthusiasts have to be up and about early and to have an eye for a good picture as Maurice Dickens captures the mood of Liverpool waterfront perfectly in this photograph of the King Orry *(5) and* Lady of Mann *(2) at the Liverpool Landing Stage.*

The **King Orry** *(5) photographed arriving at Douglas on the afternoon from Heysham, when she was painted in a livery which was almost traditional Steam Packet but the hull colour was not black and not quite Sealink blue! Consensus was that the white was far superior if not so easy to maintain which was exactly what the Company found in the 1930s when they last had vessels with white hulls. (Miles Cowsill)*

In 1998 the King Orry *(5) was surplus to requirements after eight years of excellent service. She was sold to Moby Lines for further service in the Mediterranean, renamed* Moby Love *and carried yet another somewhat spectacular livery. The vessel remains in service today. (Ferry Publications Library)*

The Steam Packet operated a subsidiary company, Mannin Line to run a freight service between Great Yarmouth and Ijmuiden chartering a Pandoro Ltd vessel **Belard** *for the service. Mannin Line purchased the vessel in 1994 but she could not maintain the schedules and sufficient traffic was not generated, as a result the venture folded. The* **Belard** *was brought to Douglas in December 1995 to operate the freight Ro-Ro service while the* **Peveril** *(4) underwent her annual survey. (Stan Basnett)*

In this photograph the two Ro-Ro freighters are together on the King Edward VIII Pier and the photograph allows a comparison of the two vessels. They were almost the same length overall but surprisingly the **Peveril** *(4) had a greater gross tonnage and not surprisingly the better sea boat. (Stan Basnett)*

The **Belard** *was back in the island again in April 1997 and is seen underway leaving Douglas for Heysham. (Miles Cowsill)*

The **Belard** *was used for a while on the Douglas/Heysham route but proved too slow which was the problem that she had on the North Sea route. She was also unpopular with the crew and soon had a reputation of rolling on the slightest swell as these three photographs taken on 2nd September 1997 show, as she leaves Douglas and immediately buries her nose on leaving the harbour mouth! (Stan Basnett)*

By 1990 Sea Containers became a majority shareholder in the Isle of Man Steam Packet and flush with the success of the **Hoverspeed Great Britain**, *Incat hull No. 025, after winning the Blue Riband for the North Atlantic crossing it was not surprising that a publicity visit was organised to promote such craft as the way to the future for sea travel. A trip up the east coast of the island was organised for politicians and Government officials. (Stan Basnett)*

When the vessel arrived the first thing that became apparent was her extreme manoeuvrability as she stopped within her own length and commenced her turn onto the berth. (Stan Basnett)

During the trip the **Peveril** *(4) was encountered inward bound for Douglas and was circled exchanging greetings before returning to Douglas ahead of her. (Stan Basnett)*

Hoverspeed Great Britain *remained berthed on the north side of the King Edward VIII Pier for the rest of the day. (Stan Basnett)*

It was to be four years before fast craft returned to Manx waters when a 74m wave piercing craft was chartered from Sea Containers to operate on the Steam Packet routes. Incat hull No. 026, the former SeaCat Boulogne, *entered service as the* SeaCat Isle of Man. *She is seen above on arrival coming alongside the Victoria Pier and below turning in the outer harbour and departing for Dublin on 24th June 1994. (Stan Basnett/Ferry Publications Library)*

SeaCat Isle of Man *continued to operate for the Steam Packet during the 1994 and 1995 seasons and is photographed leaving Douglas. The following year she did not return and was operated as* **SeaCat Norge** *for Color Line. (Stan Basnett)*

Seacat Isle of Man *photographed on 1st February 1995 in Canada Graving Dock Liverpool prior to the 1995 season. The sailings previously operated by the fast craft were covered by the* **Lady of Mann** *(2). (Dick Clague)*

We caught a glimpse of the Claymore *earlier but now we see her, while on charter to the Company, passing the head of the Victoria Pier on her entry to Douglas harbour. She is carrying a full complement of motor cycle enthusiasts coming to the island for the 1997 TT Festival. (Ferry Publications Library)*

In 1996 Sea Containers managed to obtain a controlling interest in the Steam Packet and by May had a 95% holding and the company was taken off the Stock Exchange. The following year an order for a new Ro-Pax vessel was placed with the Dutch yard of Van der Giessen-de Nord. Named the Ben my Chree *(6) she entered service in July 1998. She was the first new build for the Company since the* Lady of Mann *(2) in 1975. (Ferry Publications Library)*

The **Ben my Chree** *(6) was by far the largest ship owned by the Company and she is seen in this photograph turning in the outer harbour to set down on the new Government owned linkspan on the deepened berth on the north side of the King Edward VIII Pier. The* **King Orry** *(5) in the background, unusually berthed on the north side of the Victoria Pier, remained in service until September 1998. (Miles Cowsill)*

The Ben my Chree *(6) arrives early morning in her original livery with Laxey Towing's tug* Wendy Ann *standing by to assist. (Stan Basnett)*

Here the Ben my Chree *(6) resplendent in her new 'Steam Packet' livery and after her alterations is seen leaving Douglas with the evening sailing to Heysham on 4th March 2011. (Stan Basnett)*

A rare view of the entire fleet storm bound in Douglas harbour with the Ben my Chree *(6) berthed at the King Edward VIII Pier and the* SeaCat Isle of Mann *and* Lady of Mann *(2) at the Victoria Pier. (Stan Basnett)*

This is the morning in 1998 that the Ben my Chree *(6) arrived for the first time at Douglas. It doesn't look like a July day but it was. The first task was to undergo berthing trials at the linkspans, which she passed without problems. The lower photographs show her turning around the head of the Victoria Pier and dropping down onto the "Government" linkspan at the deepened King Edward Pier berth. (Stan Basnett)*

These two photographs of the Ben my Chree *(6) are essentially before and after photographs. Mention has already been made to the alterations made during the 1994 refit and here they can be seen to good effect. These views show her as originally delivered and below her current livery in 2011. (Miles Cowsill)*

The **Ben my Chree** *(6) has given excellent service and reliability since her introduction and has proved herself as an excellent all weather vessel sailing in all but the worst weather conditions. Any cancellations have usually been due to the exposed and difficult entry to Heysham harbour in southerly or south westerly gales. These two photographs show her leaving Douglas in a southerly gale in September 2010. (Stan Basnett)*

The Super SeaCat Two *arriving at Douglas in January 1998 in very bad weather conditions for both fuel and for berthing trials (above left) and (above right) turning in the outer harbour. She was the first of the single hull fast craft to arrive at Douglas and now showed to the full the advantage of having Sea Containers involved with the Company. Built by Fincantieri at La Spezia in Italy two years earlier she had a service speed of 38 knots and was principally used by Hoverspeed on the Liverpool-Dublin route but also for service on the Isle of Man routes. (Stan Basnett/Miles Cowsill)*

In 1999 **Super SeaCat Three** *arrived in the Island to operate on the Isle of Man routes with the Steam Packet and was also built at the Fincantieri yard. The Company embraced the use of these high speed craft and the travelling public liked the shorter journey times. Here she is leaving the Victoria Pier linkspan and again displaying the extreme manoeuvrability of these craft as she lines up to the harbour entrance. (Stan Basnett)*

Here **Super SeaCat Three** *is photographed from the 'Ben' in the Lune Channel making her approach to Heysham. (Miles Cowsill)*

This photograph by Miles Cowsill shows the beautiful lines of the Super SeaCats. They look fast, they are fast and behave like overgrown powerboats. Here the Super SeaCat Three arrives at 21.50 at Douglas on a delayed sailing from Liverpool.

Super SeaCat Three *carried a picture of Bagpuss on her bow which meant that she was referred to by many enthusiasts as just that – 'The Bagpuss'! This is another photograph of her leaving Douglas and I think she deserves better than that. (Stan Basnett)*

An evening photograph of **Super SeaCat Three** *arriving from Liverpool on 30th April 2000 and turning in the mouth of the harbour entrance, each master having his own preferred choice of where to make the turn. (Stan Basnett)*

The 74m **SeaCat Danmark**, *incat hull No. 027, was on charter to the Steam Packet in 1998 from Hoverspeed and is seen in this photograph off the east coast of the island on a Belfast-Douglas sailing. (Stan Basnett)*

During 2006 the 81m SeaCat Diamant*, Incat hull No. 041, was on charter from Hoverspeed and sporting a very patriotic livery. She was taken on by the Steam Packet to assist with the heavy traffic during the TT period. Here she is just leaving the Victoria Pier berth with a Liverpool sailing on 3rd June 2006. (Stan Basnett)*

Another view of **SeaCat Diamant** *just after the one on the previous page that shows the size of these 81m wave piercing craft. It also illustrates that immediately on leaving the Victoria Pier linkspan vessels have to move to the middle of the outer harbour in order to make a port hand turn to line up for the harbour mouth. (Stan Basnett)*

The **SeaCat Scotland** *Incat hull No. 028, was yet another of the Incat 74m wave piercing high speed craft to be used by the Steam Packet on their Irish Sea route during the 1997 and 1998 season and the craft is seen approaching the berth at Belfast in these two photographs. (Maurice Dickens)*

We saw several of the smaller fast craft at Douglas during this initial period of operation of the high speed services and it was hard to keep up with the various vessels employed as they tended to change their names dependent on the service they had previously operated. The Sea Express 1, *Incat hull No. 026, arrived in 2006 after an extensive refit at Birkenhead and berthed at the Victoria Pier, she had previously been* SeaCat Isle of Man. *During the early part of 2007 the craft was involved in a collision with* Alaska Rainbow *in the Mersey. (Stan Basnett)*

Many of the 74m fast craft appeared under different names and to help keep track of them the hull number is also included. The Emeraude France *(hull No. 023), normally operated by Emeraude Ferries on cross-channel routes, was chartered by the Steam Packet for the 2007 season. The photograph shows the craft in a most unusual location berthed at the ferry steps on the Battery Pier at Douglas. (Stan Basnett)*

The **Emeraude France** *arrived at Douglas on 19th May after a month in dry dock at Birkenhead ready for the busy TT traffic still carrying the Emeraude Ferries logo on her side. She operated a day trip to Whitehaven in August establishing what must be a record for the shortest sea crossing to England, in the process taking an hour for the journey. (Stan Basnett)*

The 91m P&O **Express**, *Incat hull No. 047, normally operating the Larne/Cairnryan service for P&O, was chartered to provide additional capacity from Northern Island for the TT where there is a huge following of motorcycle racing. Sailings were from Larne to Douglas and supplemented the Company's Belfast sailings. These sailings had to be accommodated within her normal schedule which meant arrivals were usually in the middle of the night. This is her 05.30 departure from Douglas on the 31st May! (Stan Basnett)*

The 81m **Rapide**, *Incat hull No. 038, was another wave piercing Incat vessel which was put on service between Douglas and Liverpool and is just leaving the Victoria Pier. (Stan Basnett)*

A stern view of **Rapide** *showing the twin ramps to the vehicle deck and another illustration of the need for vessels leaving the Victoria Pier linkspan to give clearance of the pier to execute the necessary port hand turn to leave the harbour. (Stan Basnett)*

SeaCat Scotland, *Incat hull No. 028, another 74m wave piercing vessel is berthed at the Victoria Pier pre-season for essential maintenance to be carried out by Fort Street Engineering which is the engineering arm of the Steam Packet. (Stan Basnett)*

It is perhaps difficult for those who have not been to the Island during TT fortnight to understand the impact it has. The Island's population doubles, there are more vehicles and motorcycles moving to and from the island and there is an increase in demand for food. This is why we see freight vessels being chartered to assist with backlogs that inevitably occur as we have seen already. In this sequence we see the Douglas harbour pilot Capt. Stephen Carter heading out and boarding the East Express *approaching Douglas on 9th June 2008. (Stan Basnett)*

Now we have an opportune moment to look at some of the other freight vessels that the Steam Packet have had on charter in recent times. CFF Seine, *owned by Clarkson Ferries of Glasgow, was on service in March 2006 to cover for the* Ben my Chree *(6). These freight Ro-Ro vessels were some of the largest to use the harbour at Douglas. She had been at Douglas earlier as* Dart 1. *(Stan Basnett)*

March 2010 saw the Clipper Ranger *at Douglas on charter from Seatruck. (Stan Basnett)*

P&O Irish Sea's European Mariner *being available was on charter to the Steam Packet in January 2002 to cover the refit of the* Ben My Chree *(6). (Stan Basnett)*

The **Stena Caledonia** *was chartered on several occasions by the Steam Packet during TT fortnight. Here is she seen leaving Douglas harbour bound for Heysham. (Miles Cowsill)*

In 2008 the Steam Packet undertook a re-branding exercise and the fleet appeared for the first time for years in the same livery and for traditionalists it was a welcome sight, but at the same time very modern, carrying the website address on the side of the black hull. The company logo also reverted to carrying the full Isle of Man Steam Packet title. The fast craft mono hull Super SeaCat Two *rejoined the fleet, now renamed as the* Viking *(2) and is seen just leaving the Victoria pier linkspan. (Stan Basnett)*

This sequence shows the snake-like departure from Douglas following the extension of the breakwater and the new approach channel. The Viking *(2) completes her departure on 23rd August 2008 and clears her manifolds as the engines are opened up. All a bit reminiscent of her namesake! (Stan Basnett)*

I make no apologies for including these two photographs of the Viking (2) *that show the classy lines reflecting perhaps some of the Italian flair in her design – the Ferrari of the fast craft. The monohull at speed is like travelling in a powerboat in slow-mo! Some didn't like it but I unashamedly did, perhaps the engine mountings didn't! The bow shot of her at her berth just breathes speed as does the profile photograph below as she passes Clay Head on the approach to Douglas on 9th June 2008. (Stan Basnett)*

The Steam Packet sold the **Viking** *(2) the following year to make way for their purchase of Incat hull No.050. She made a last appearance early in 2009 on the Irish Sea to cover for the 'Ben's' dry docking before being sold to Hellenic Seaways and renamed* **Hellenic Wind**. *She is photographed in April 2011 at Ponta Delgada on the island of São Miguel in the Azores operated by Atlânticoline still looking very much a Steam Packet ship and fitted with a side-loading door! (Stan Basnett)*

Incat hull No. 026 appeared back on the island resplendent in the new, and by far the best, livery. She was renamed Snaefell *(6). Previously she had been Sea Containers'* SeaCat Isle of Man. *She is photographed on 9th June 2008 off Douglas Head. (Stan Basnett)*

The Snaefell *(6) ran a day trip to Belfast in August 2008 and called at Peel maybe becoming the last Steam Packet vessel to call there? (Doug Allen)*

In 2002 Incat hull No. 050 entered a joint venture between Bollinger/Incat USA and the US Joint Forces Command for 24 months to evaluate the suitability of wave piercing fast craft for use in the rapid deployment of troops and equipment world wide. Fitted with a helicopter deck aft sher became Joint Venture HSV–X1 *and there followed extensive trials in all weather conditions including winter crossings of the Atlantic. (Incat)*

On completion of her military evaluation with the US Army, Incat hull No.050 was offered for sale and taken up eventually by the Steam Packet and following an extensive refit entered service with the company in 2009 as the Manannan *named after the island's mythical god of the sea. (Stan Basnett)*

The Manannan *became the largest high speed craft operating in the Irish Sea on introduction in 2009 and proved her worth maintaining schedules in weather that earlier would have seen fast craft sailings cancelled. She is approaching Douglas on 19th July 2011 from Dublin passing m.t.* Sarpen *anchored off Douglas awaiting the abatement of a north-westerly gale. (Stan Basnett)*

This photograph shows the single lane loading ramp fitted to Manannan *as she leaves Douglas on 7th March 2010. This and the method of loading and unloading foot passengers on heavy loadings are the only criticisms of the craft which no doubt in time will be addressed. (Stan Basnett)*

The **Manannan** *is without doubt the pride of the fleet and is extremely popular for the level of comfort afforded to passengers having a bar, cafeteria and two cinemas in addition to three lounges, two of which are select. She is seen here turning in the outer harbour on 7th March 2010. (Stan Basnett)*

The **Manannan***'s regular route is Douglas to Liverpool and this is the other end of her journey as she approaches the Liverpool Landing Stage. (Roy Cressey)*